InDesign CC - Creating Brochures
A Step-By-Step Training Guide

InDesign is the desktop publishing industry standard used to develop marketing brochures and catalogs.

This manual will be used to help design artwork for brochures, printing, or displaying on the web. InDesign is perfect for illustrations, brochures, and single page artwork. In this course, students will work with tools and features for the creation of high-quality precision design layouts, and use selection capability to manipulate frames and objects within frames. Two very important tools used to adjust the image and the frames are the "Selection" and the "Direct Select" tools. Other important aspects are the "Master Pages" that can be used to create headers, footers, watermarks, or any object placed on the design to appear on multiple pages. During class, students will not only create a single brochure, but also a four-page brochure that will combine all the concepts of the class into a viable learning experience. Commands are provided for **InDesign CC, CS6,** and **InDesign Mac CS6.**

Table of Contents
Chapter 1 - Interface / Menu Overview 4
    Section 1: Core Concepts 4
    Section 2: Optional Concepts..7
Chapter 2 - Common Capabilities 8
    Section 1: Core Concepts 8
    Section 2: Optional Concepts..10
Chapter 3 - New Document 12
    Section 1: Core Concepts 12
    Section 2: Optional Concepts..14
Chapter 4 - Text Threading and Graphics Placement 16
    Section 1: Core Concepts 16
    Section 2: Optional Concepts..18
Chapter 5 - Master Page..21
    Section 1: Core Concepts 21
    Section 2: Optional Concepts..23
Index - InDesign CC Creating Brochures..30

Student Projects
Student Project A - Surewood Realty Project...11
Student Project B - Healthy Dining Selections...19
Student Project C - Four Page Newsletter...25

About the Author

Jeff Hutchinson is a computer instructor teaching a variety of classes around the country. He has a BS degree from BYU in Computer-Aided Engineering and has worked in the Information Technology field supporting and maintaining computers for many years. He also previously owned a computer training and consulting firm in San Francisco, California. After selling his business in 2001, he has continued to work as an independent computer instructor/consultant around the country. Jeff Hutchinson lives in Utah and also provides training for Utah Valley University Community Education system, offering valuable computer skills for the general knowledge of students, career development, and career advancement. Understanding the technology and the needs of students has been the basis for developing this material. Jeff Hutchinson can be contacted at jeffhutch@elearnlogic.com or (801) 376-6687.

Copyright and Release Information

This workbook/guide has been updated on **9/15/2017 (Version 4)** and is designed for **Adobe InDesign CS6** and **CC**. Also, **Mac CS6** commands are added due to the keyboard and menu differences. This guide is the sole property of Jeff Hutchinson and **eLearnLogic.** Any emailing, copying, duplication or reproduction of this guide, must be approved by Jeff Hutchinson in writing. However, students who take a class or purchase the guide are free to use it for personal development and learning.
ISDN-13: 978-1976466694

Introduction

Exercise Download

Exercises are posted on the web site and can be downloaded to your computer. Please do the following:

Open Internet Explorer/Edge: Or Google Chrome:

Type the web address:

elearnlogic.com/download/indesigncc-1.exe

You might get several security warnings, but answer yes and run through each one. When you click "**Unzip**," the files will be located in **C:\Data\InDesignCC-1** folder.

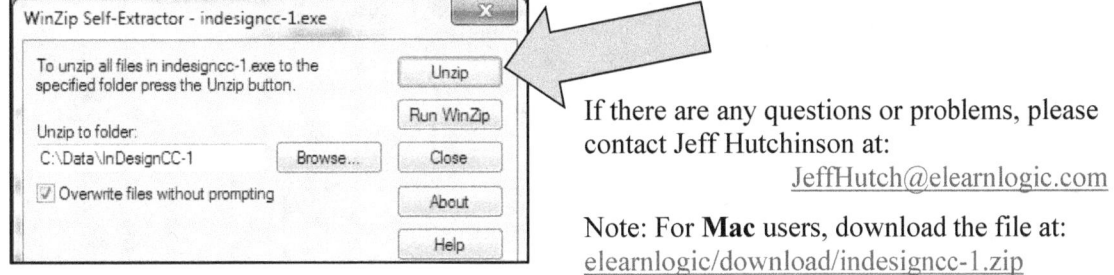

If there are any questions or problems, please contact Jeff Hutchinson at:

JeffHutch@elearnlogic.com

Note: For **Mac** users, download the file at:
elearnlogic/download/indesigncc-1.zip

Design Strategy

This workbook is designed in conjunction with an Online-Instructor-Led course (for more information see: www.elearnlogic.com). Unlike other computer guides, students will not need to review lengthy procedures in order to understand a topic. All that is necessary are the brief statements and command paths located within the guide that demonstrate how a concept is used. There are many **Step-By-Step Practice Exercises** and more comprehensive **Student Projects** used to better understand a concept. Furthermore, students will find that this workbook guide is often used as a reference to help users understand concepts quickly. An index is also provided on the last page of the workbook to reference important topics as necessary. However, if more detail is needed for study, the Internet can be used to search a concept. Also, if student's skills are weak due to lack of use, they can refresh their knowledge quickly by visually scanning the concept needed and then testing them out using the application.

Manual Organization

The following are special formatting conventions:
- **Numbered Sections** on the left are the **Concepts** covered.
- **Italic Text** is used to highlight commands that will perform the **Concept** or procedure in completing the practice exercises.
- **Practice Exercises** are a **Step-by-Step** approach to demonstrate the **Concept.**
- **Student Projects** are a more comprehensive approach to demonstrate the **Concept.**
- **Dark, Grayed-Out Sections** are optional/advanced **Concepts.**
- **Bolded** items are important **Concepts,** terminology or commands used.
- **Tip** - These are additional ideas about the **Concept.**

InDesign CC - Creating Brochures

Chapter 1 - Interface / Menu Overview

If you are new to InDesign, you will need to familiarize yourself with the basic features of the program. We will first look at the interface and the basic navigation features. The interface is different from other applications, and understanding its layout and components is vital to using the program effectively.

Chapter Contents:
- Section 1: Core Concepts
- Section 2: Optional Concepts

Section 1: Core Concepts

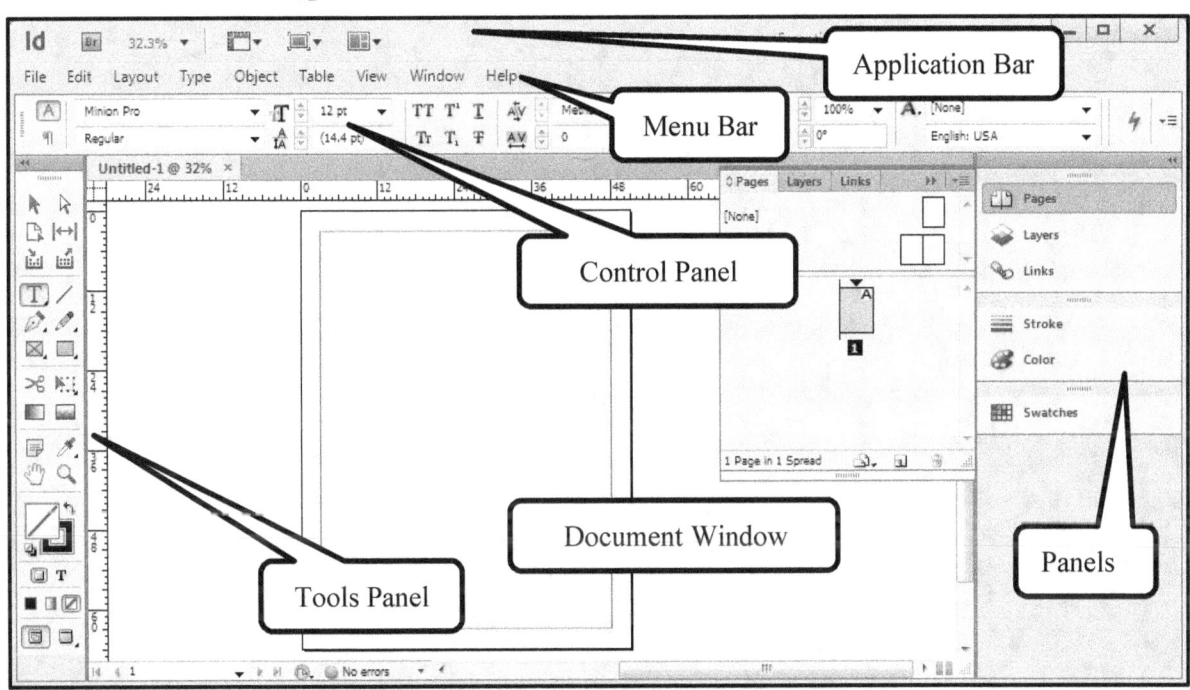

Concept	Explanation / *Command String in italic.*			
1.1 Exercises	Exercise files on a **PC** are located at **C:\Data\InDesignCC-All** folder and the **Mac** files are usually stored on the desktop in the **InDesignCC-All** folder.			
Practice Exercise 1 Open file	**Open Blank Document:** *File Menu→New→Document→ Document Preset: Default.*			
1.2 Mac Keyboard Commands	There are a few fundamental differences to identify: **Ctrl Key** (used in MS Windows) = **Command Key** (used on the **Mac**). **Alt Key** (used in MS Windows) = **Option Key** (used on the **Mac**). *Edit Menu→Preferences (used in MS Windows)* = ***InDesign→Preferences (Mac)***			
1.3 Adobe Terminology	**Industry Term** = **Adobe Term**		**Industry Term** = **Adobe Term**	
	Text	= Type	Special Characters =	Glyphs
	Border	= Stroke	Transparency =	Opacity
	Insert	= Place	Color Samples =	Swatches

Chapter 1 - Interface / Menu Overview

1.4 Menu Bar	The **Menu Bar** is located on the top of the interface and contains menus such as *File*, *Edit*, *Layout*, *Type*, *Object*, *Table*, *View window,* and ***help***.	
1.5 Tools Panel	This is located on the left side and contains many tools used to manipulate objects on the document window. Some of the more common commands are **Selection** tools (**Selection** and **Direct Selection** tools), **Zooming**, and **Manipulation** tools.	
1.6 Control Panel	Students can quickly access options and commands related to the tools chosen (tools are located on the left side of the screen). Each tool displays a different control panel. This gives you the necessary adjustment for the tool provided.	
1.7 Panels	These are located on the right side of the screen and contain the valuable options necessary to manipulate objects on the screen. Some **Panels** are used to status information and some are used to set valuable tool defaults such **Page, Text Wrap, Links, Color, Swatches, and Stroke**. The panels can be laid out in **floating, docked**, or **fly out** panel modes.	
1.8 Document Window	This is where your design is placed and you can manipulate the objects to produce your end result. The Pasteboard is the area outside the page area and can be used to place objects prior to moving them to your design.	
1.9 Status Bar	Probably the most significant aspect of the **Status bar** is the **Preflight errors.** This can be used to identify possible problems with your design layout such as text that falls outside of the frame. You can also open: *Window→Output→Preflight* to see these errors.	
1.10 Workspace	*Window Menu→Workspace→New Workspace.*	
1.11 Menu	This will allow you to color code and remove menu items. ***Edit Menu→Menus.*** 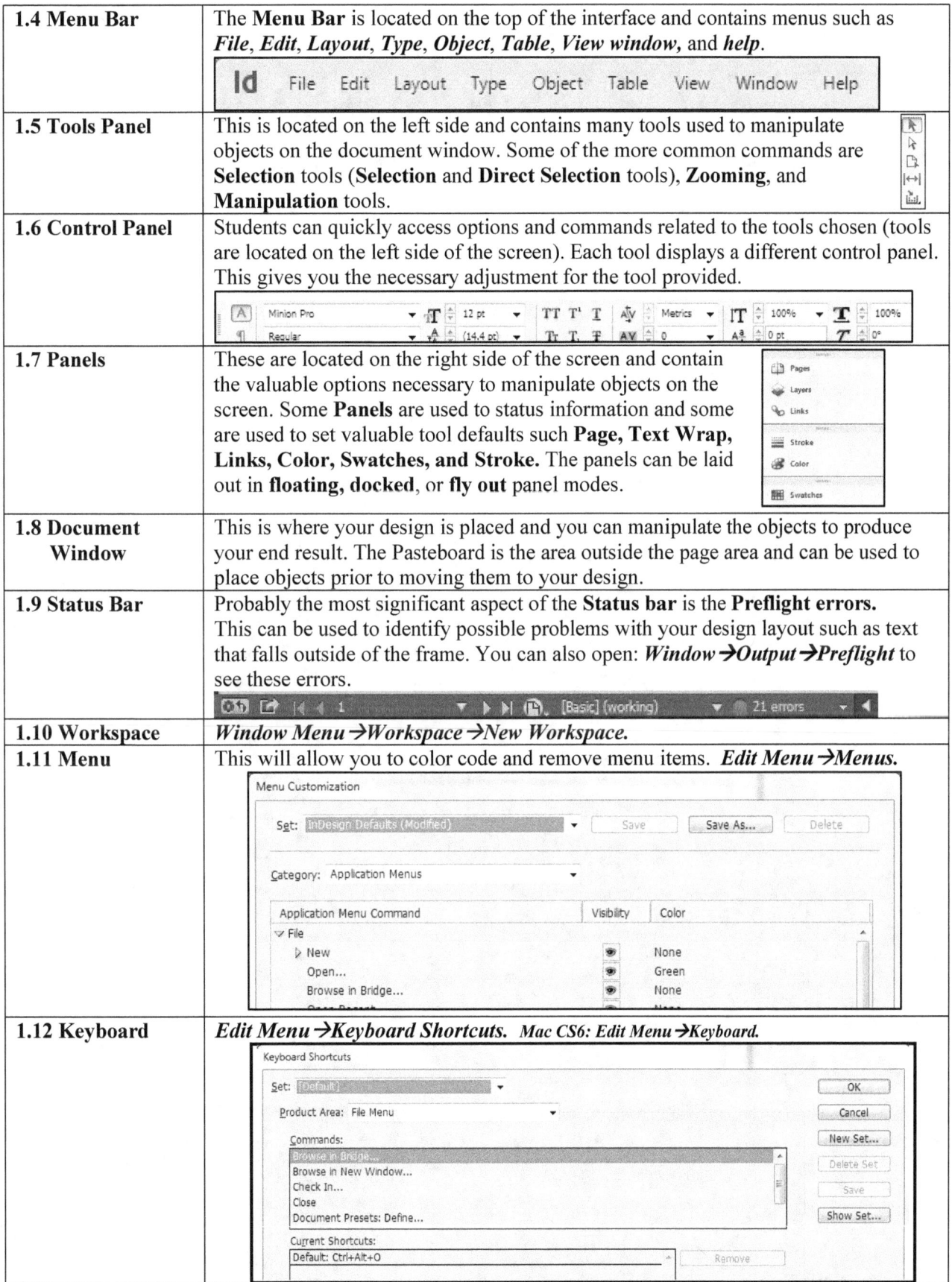
1.12 Keyboard	***Edit Menu→Keyboard Shortcuts.*** Mac CS6: *Edit Menu→Keyboard.*

Page 5

Chapter 1 - Interface / Menu Overview

Practice Exercise 2	*Undo=Ctrl Z, Redo=Shift+Ctrl+Z, Open=Ctrl W, Exit=Ctrl Q*
1.13 Preferences	These are default options or ways the program behaves to the command chosen. *Edit Menu →* *Preferences →General.* Mac CS6: *InDesign Menu →* *Preferences →General*
1.14 Selection Tool	▶ This selects and manipulates a frame. Press **Shift** with the selection tool to add to/delete from the selection. Draw a box to select a group of objects.
1.15 Direct Selection Tool	▶ This manipulates the image within a frame. In the middle of every image, there is a transparent Bulls Eye ⊙ (see right side). The **Direct Selection** mode is chosen to modify the image within the frame.
Practice Exercise 3	*File Tab→Place →B-Gale Hunter.jpg →(Place it anywhere) Selection Tool→Move the graphic frame→Direct Select Tool→Move the graphic image inside the frame.*
Practice Exercise 4	**Continue from the previous Practice Exercise.** *Selection Tool→Click on the Bulls Eye in the middle of the image→Move the image inside the frame.* Note: you are using the Direct Select tool.
1.16 Zooming	**Zoom out:** *Zoom Tool* 🔍 *→Hold the Alt Key→Click the window* (Mac CS6: Use the **Option Key** instead of the **Alt Key**). **Zoom in:** *Ctrl +* (Mac CS6: Use the **Command +**). **Zoom out:** *Ctrl -* (Mac CS6: Use the **Command -**). **Full screen:** *Ctrl 0* (Mac CS6: Use the **Command 0**). **Zoom out:** *Ctrl-Space Bar* (Mac CS6: Use the **Command space bar**). **Zoom in:** *Ctrl Alt-Space Bar* (Mac CS6: Use the **Options Command space bar**). *Hold Alt Key →Mouse roller* to zoom in/out. **Power Zoom -** *Hand Tool→Hold Left Mouse Button→Move the Arrow Key* to *change the red zoom box. Supported in version CS4+.* **Mouse Wheel:** *Roll the wheel to zoom in or out.* Power Zoom. **Note:** The **Navigator Panel** was discontinued in CS4.
1.17 View Commands	**Text Threads:** *View Menu→Extras→Show Text Threads / Hide Text Threads.* **Guides:** *View Menu→Grids & Guides→Hide Guides / Show Guides.* **Ruler:** *View Menu→Hide Rulers / Show Rulers.* **Frame:** *View Menu→Extras→Show Frame Edges / Hide Frame Edges.* **Preview:** *View Menu→Screen Mode→Preview / Normal.*
1.18 Guides	Drag the **Guide** from the ruler to the layout. To move the **Guide**, hold the **Ctrl Key** down. Mac CS6: Use the **Command Key**. To delete the **Guide**, hold the **Ctrl Key** down and press the **Delete Key**. Mac CS6: Use the **Command Key**.
1.19 Rulers	*View Menu→Show Rulers/Hide Rulers.*

Chapter 1 - Interface / Menu Overview

1.20 Smart Guides	When two objects are manually aligned, green alignment lines will appear allowing for the **center, top, or bottom** alignment of the objects.	
Practice Exercise 5	Continue from the previous exercise. Make sure all images are unselected and then insert another image in order to see the smart guides. ***File Tab→Place→B-House For Sale.jpg→(Place the image anywhere)→Move the image to align with Image 1→Review the green Smart Guides.***	

Practice Exercise 6 - Reviewing the Interface

The purpose of this project is to test the selection tools and learn to navigate through the pages.
1. ***File Menu→Open→Schedule.indd***
2. Selection Techniques
   a. Select the following picture on page 2 by choosing the **Selection Tool** and adjusting the picture.
   b. Move the frame of the picture.
   c. Choose the **Direct Selection Tool**.
   d. Move the picture (notice it moves within the frame).
3. Zoom Techniques
   a. Choose the **Zoom Tool**  on the left side at the bottom of the screen.
   b. Click an object to zoom in and use the **Alt Key** to zoom out.
   c. Hold the **Ctrl Key** and type **0** (the number zero) on the keyboard.
      (*Mac CS6: Use the **Command Key** and **0***)
   d. Try some of the other zoom techniques outlined in this chapter.
4. Menu adjustments:
   a. ***Edit Menu→Menus→File→Turn off the eye.***

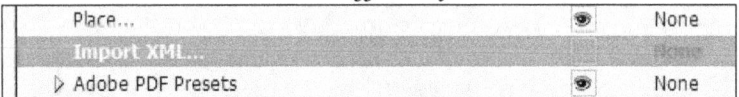

   b. Highlight the **Open** command in the **File Menu**.

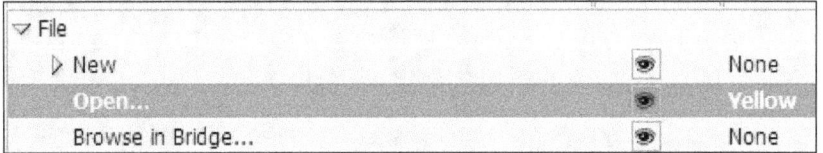

Section 2: Optional Concepts

1.21 Application Bar Available CS4+	This is located on the very top edge of the interface window. It contains **Magnification View, Screen Mode Options,** and the **Arrange Documents** drop-down list.
1.22 Display Performance	***Edit Menu→Preferences→General*** or ***R-Click on Image→Display Performance→High-Quality Display***. *Mac CS6: **InDesign Menu→Preferences→General**. No Right-Click available on **Mac**.*
1.23 Dictionary	***Edit Menu→Preferences→Dictionary→New User Dictionary Icon***. To add a word to a dictionary: ***Edit Menu→Spelling→Dictionary*** or ***Select word→R-Click→Spelling→User Dictionary***. *Mac CS6: **InDesign Menu→Preferences→Dictionary**.*

Chapter 2 - Common Capabilities

We will now review the common capabilities provided to complete the projects contained in this courseware. Open **InDesign** and start a new blank document using the default parameters.

Chapter Contents:
Section 1: Core Concepts
Section 2: Optional Concepts

Section 1: Core Concepts

Concept	Explanation / *Command String in italic.*
Practice Exercise 7 Open Blank Doc	**Open Blank Document:** *File Menu→New→Document→ Document Preset: Default.*
2.1 Placing Text/Graphics	Place objects and text: *File Menu→Place.* View import options: *File Menu→Place→ ☑ Show Import Options.* The next time you place an image, you can uncheck ☐ the import options.
Practice Exercise 8 Placement	Place something: *File Menu→Place→ B-House2.jpg.*
2.2 Frames	All objects and text are bound within a frame. They can be moved and manipulated independently and as a group.
2.3 Type Tool	T. This is the standard tool used to add text. *Type Tool→Draw a box→Type the text.*
2.4 Type on a Path	This will type text on a path using the **Pencil, Pin** or **Shapes.** *Ellipse Tool→Draw Ellipse→Type on a Path Tool→Click on the edge of the ellipse and type the text.*
2.5 Line Tool	Lines are usually drawn at a 0 width. Therefore, you must apply a width. The **Shift Key** draws 45° angles. The **Alt Key** draws from the center. *Line Tool→Hold the Shift Key→Draw the Line.*
2.6 Rectangle Tool	The **Shift Key** draws a perfect square. The **Alt Key** draws from the center. *Rectangle Tool→Hold the Shift Key→Draw the rectangle.* Mac CS6: Use the **Option Key**.
Practice Exercise 9 Draw Rectangle	*Rectangle Tool→Draw a rectangle.* Use the **Alt** and the **Shift Keys**.
2.7 Ellipse Tool	The **Shift Key** draws a perfect circle. The **Alt Key** draws from the center. *Ellipse Tool→Hold the Shift Key→Draw the Ellipse.* Mac CS6: Use the **Option Key**.
Practice Exercise 10 Draw on a Path	*Ellipse Tool→Draw an Ellipse→Text on a Path Tool→Click on the path of the Ellipse→Type the text.* Note: Look for the + that appears in the cursor.
2.8 Polygon Tool	The **Shift Key** draws a perfect polygon. The **Alt Key** draws from the center. *Polygon Tool→Hold the Shift Key→Draw the Polygon.* Mac CS6: Use the **Option Key**.
2.9 Hand Tool	This is used to move the page. *Hand Tool→Click on the page→Move the page.* The hand tool is considered a neutral tool and can be used to terminate the use of another tool such as the line tool.
Practice Exercise 11	*Line Tool →(Draw a line)→Click the Hand Tool when finished.*
2.10 Zoom Tool	Press the **Alt Key** to zoom in or draw a box around the area. *Note: Mac CS6: Use the Options Key to zoom out.*

Chapter 2 - Common Capabilities

2.11 Color Panel	Color This will change the color of a text frame or text. *Window Menu → Color.*	
2.12 Color Picker	This is located in **Tools** and is used to fill the background of a frame or apply stroke with color.	
2.13 Strokes Panel	This is used to add borders to a frame. Stroke The **Strokes Panel** is used to place thick borders around a frame. *Window Menu →Stroke.*	
Practice Exercise 12 Color Picker	**Fill Text Box Red:** *Select Text box→Click the Color picker/Show the Fill →Color Red.* Place a Blue Stroke around the text box: *Select Text box→Click the Color picker/Show the Outline →Color Blue.*	
2.14 Swatches Panel	Swatches This will store a common set of colors created from the **Eye Dropper Tool** or **Color Panel**. *Window Menu →Swatches.*	
2.15 Copy Frame	This method is easier than the copy & paste technique. *Selection Tool→Select Frame→Alt Key →Drag n Drop.* **Mac CS6:** *Use the Options Key.*	
2.16 Proportional	This will adjust the image to fit the frame. *Selection Tool→Select Frame→Shift→Move corners.*	
2.17 Frame Handles	These are small circles or handles used to change the size of the text frame.	Handle
2.18 Rotate	*Select object→Object Menu→Transform→Rotate or Rotate Tool.* Use the selection tool and the rotation cursor will appear outside the frame handle (see rotation symbol in the picture to the right).	Rotate
Practice Exercise 13 Rotate Image	*File Menu →Place → B-House3.jpg* Rotate a graphic image: *Select Image →Object Menu →Rotate or grab the rotation angle just outside of the round handle.*	
2.19 Special Characters	*Type Menu→Insert Special Character→Symbols→Trademark Symbol* or *Type Menu→Glyphs.* **Mac CS6:** *Insert→Special Character.*	T T™
2.20 Vertical Justification	*Select Object →Object Menu→Text Frame Options Vertical Justification→Center.* *The end result →*	Title
Practice Exercise 14 Text Box	*Text Tool →Draw box→Type text →Type Menu→Insert Special Character→Symbols→Trademark Symbol*	

Page 9

Chapter 2 - Common Capabilities

2.21 Stacking Order	This will change which object is on top and on the bottom. ***Right-Click on any Object →Arrange →Bring to Front.***	
2.22 Converting Shapes	This will convert the frame to a different shape. ***Select Object →Object Menu →Convert Shape →Ellipse.***	
2.23 Fit A Frame	This will adjust the image to fit in the frame. ***Select Object →Object Menu →Fitting → Fill Frame Proportionally.*** (Fit Content to Frame)	
2.24 Grouping Objects	This will group two frames so they can be selected and moved together. ***Select Objects →Object Menu →Group.***	
Practice Exercise 15 Manipulation	***File Menu →Place →Select B-House2.jpg and B-House3.jpg → Open →Test Stacking order, Converting shapes, Fit a Frame, and Grouping objects.***	
2.25 Eye Dropper	🖉. This samples the color and text formatting and then allows you to paste by selecting new items after sampling.	
Practice Exercise 16	***File Menu →Place →B-Inside2.jpg →Eye Dropper Tool 🖉 →Eye drop the wood cabinets →Window →Swatch Panel →New Swatch.***	
Practice Exercise 17	***File Menu →Open →Schedule.indd →Eye Dropper Tool 🖉 →select the word "Hands-On" →format the blue text by selecting the blue text.***	
2.26 Accelerate Movement	The movement of the object will be accelerated when you press the **Shift** Key and the **Arrow Keys**. ***Select Object →Hold the Shift Key down →Down Arrow Key.***	

Section 2: Optional Concepts

2.27 Margins and Columns	To change the margins and columns after you create a page: ***Layout Menu → Margins and Columns.***	
2.28 Document Setup	To change the page size, facing pages, width, height, bleed and slug after you create a page: ***File Menu →Document Setup.***	
2.29 Screen Mode	Similar to print preview: ***View →Screen Mode →Preview.***	

Student Project A - Surewood Realty Project

1. **Open InDesign CS6 or CC.**
2. Create a new document and choose the following options: **Page Size: Letter, Orientation: Portrait, All Margins: .25 in**
3. The graphic files are located in the InDesignCC-All folder and the file names start with the word "A." Use the *File Menu→Place* to place the following graphics:

The completed version is called: **C:\Data\InDesignCC-All\A-Surewood Realtors.pdf**

Chapter 3 - New Document

Creating a new document is usually the first thing you will do.

      Chapter Contents:
           Section 1: Core Concepts
           Section 2: Optional Concepts

Section 1: Core Concepts

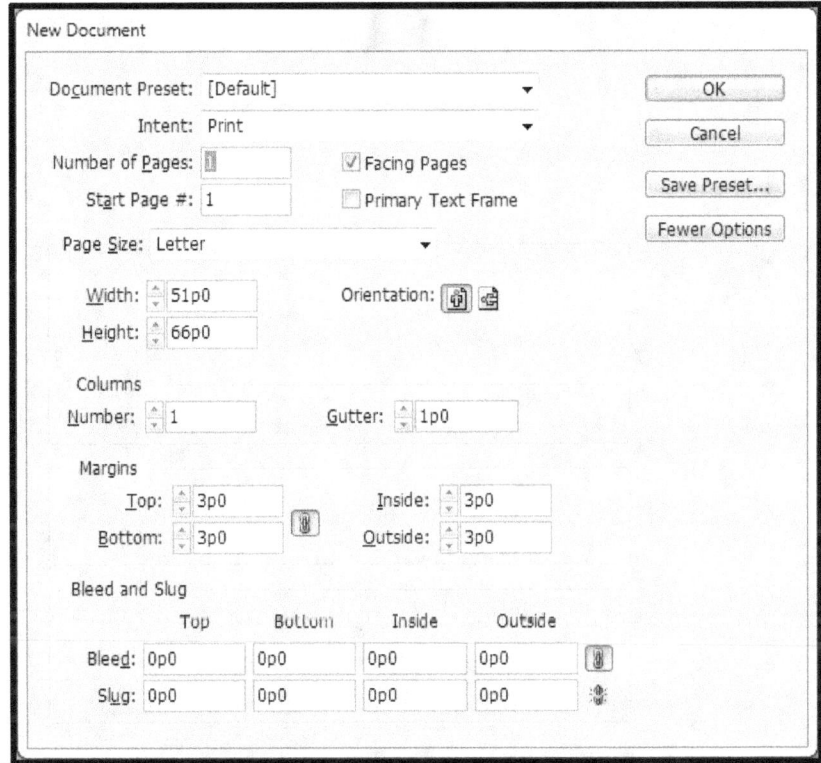

Concept	Explanation / *Command String in italic.*
3.1 New Document	**Open Blank Document:** *File Menu→New→Document*.
3.2 Document Presets	This is a drop-down list that allows you to enter a name to customize a document.
3.3 Intent	This changes the setting in the new document dialog box if the final result is **Print, Web** or **Digital Publishing**.
3.4 Number of pages	This is a text box that allows you to enter the number of pages in a document.
3.5 Start Page #	This is the starting page number.
3.6 ☑ Facing Pages	This sets the layout to be a two-page spread like a book.
3.7 Save Preset	This allows you to save the preset or information typed on the screen for future use.

Chapter 3 - New Document

3.8 Fewer/More Options	This contains the **Bleed** and **Slug** information. See below for detailed descriptions.	

3.9 Page Size	Page Size - This is a drop-down list that enables you to select the page type and specify the width and height of the page. You can set the orientation of the page to either **Portrait** or **Landscape**.
	 A **Pica** (pronounced with a long "I" sound) is a typographic unit of measure to 1/6th of an inch. The **Pica** contains 12-point units of measure. It originated around the year 1785 when Françoise Ambrose Didot (1730-1804) refined the typographic measures system:
	     72 points=1 inch
	     6picas= 1 inch
	     1 Pica = 12 Points
	 Note: You can also type in 1 inch instead of 6P0.	

3.10 Width	This is the width of the page.	
3.11 Height	This is the height of the page.	
3.12 Orientation	This is Portrait or Landscape orientation.	
3.13 Columns	This is a section that allows you to specify the number of columns and also the space between each column.	
3.14 Gutter	This is the space between the columns.	
3.15 Margins	This is a section that allows you to specify the **top, bottom, inside, and outside** margins in a document. If linked, all values will change together. Margin layout when Facing Pages is checked. Inside is between documents. Margin layout when Facing Pages is not checked. Margins are outside the column area.	
3.16 Bleed	This extends the graphic image beyond the edge of the page into the bleed area. When printed, the physical print area will be a nice, straight line. The bleed extends outside the page. If linked, all values will change together. When Facing Pages is checked, you can bleed inside the fold of facing pages.	

Chapter 3 - New Document

3.17 Slug	This area will hold non-printed information such as **date, time,** and **release label** information. It is usually never printed and used for reference only. If linked, all values will change together. The version can be identified on the document.

Section 2: Optional Concepts

3.18 Primary Text Frame	This will automatically place a text frame on the A Master and thread it between the pages. It creates a primary text frame if checked, or not checked. *File Menu→New →Document →✓ Primary Text Frame*.
3.19 Inches Vs Pica	*Edit Menu→Preferences →Unit & Measure →Change to inches.* *Mac CS6: InDesign Menu →Preferences.*

New Page Layout

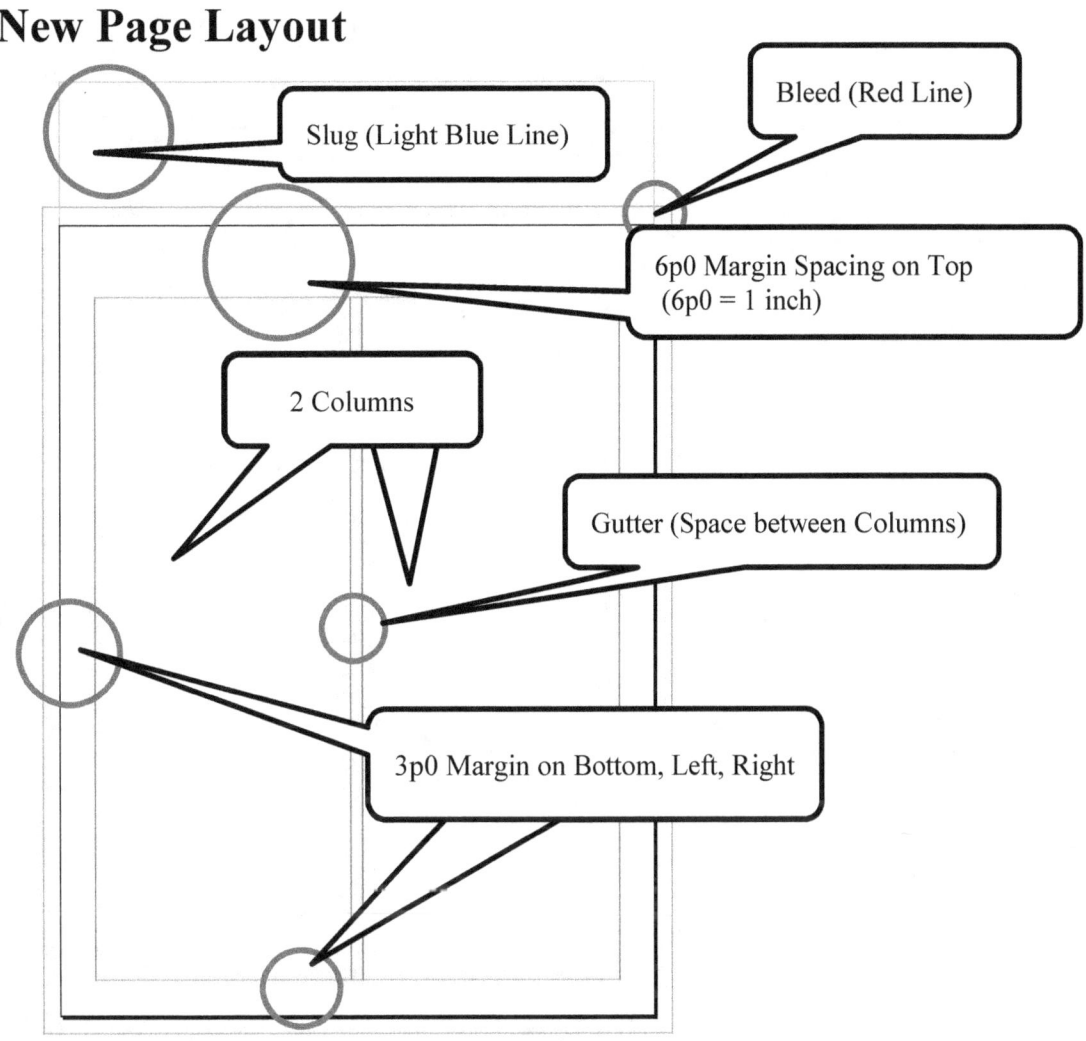

Practice Exercise 18 - New Document
1. Create a new document and save the precepts as **MyNewLayout.**
2. Create a **business card** 3in. x 2in.
3. Create a **postcard** 4in. x 6in.
4. Create a **greeting card** 4.25in. x 5.5in., 4-page foldout, facing pages.
   Select Page1, Uncheck option "Allow Document pages to shuffle"(→Uncheck), More options →Insert Pages→ Insert: Before Page.
5. Create a **6-page brochure**, 8.5in x 11in, facing pages.

Chapter 4 - Text Threading and Graphics Placement

Text Threading is a fundamental part of InDesign. It allows text to flow from column to column or page to page. You can start a story in one column and continue the story elsewhere in the document. Open **InDesign** and start a new blank document with the following parameters:

Chapter Contents:
    Section 1: Core Concepts
    Section 2: Optional Concepts

Section 1: Core Concepts

Concept	Explanation / *Command String in italic.*
Practice Exercise 19 Open New Document	Open Blank Document: *File Menu→New→Document→ Document Preset: Default.*
Practice Exercise 20	*File Menu→Place→ D3-Restaurants.docx.*
4.1 Manual Text Threading	**Threading** will tie a large article across multiple frames. Select the **Red Box** in the lower left corner of the frame and create a continuation frame. *File Menu →Place →Text Filename → Pickup Overset text in the lower right Corner→Draw new text frame location.*
4.2 Simi-Automatic Text Threading ALT Key	When you keep the **Alt Key** down, you can draw continuation frames as long as the article continues. *File Menu →Place →Text Filename→Hold Alt Draw the text box →Alt-Draw the text box →Alt-Draw the text box →Alt-Draw the text box.* **Mac CS6:** *Use the* **Option Key.**
4.3 Automatic Text Threading Shift Key	By holding the **Shift Key** down, additional frames can be created as needed. *File Menu →Place →Text Filename →Shift Key →Place on page 1* Note: The text will flow to multiple pages. **Mac CS6:** *Use the* **Shift Key.**
4.4 Thread Between Text Boxes	This will show the line connecting the frames. *View Menu →Extras →Show Text Threads. / Hide Text Threads.* You can break threads by double-clicking on a thread connection point.
4.5 Selection	To select, use the mouse button: **Double Click**=Selects a word. **Triple Click**=Selects a row of text. **Quad Clicks**=Selects a paragraph. **5 Clicks**=Selects the entire thread.
4.6 Story Editor	The **Story Editor** allows you to view the entire article thread and allows for easy reading, spelling and grammar checking. To open the **Story Editor**: *Select the text frame →Type Tool →Select Text →R-Click → Edit in Story Editor Or Edit Menu→Edit in Story Editor.* You can also **Spell Check** within the **Story Editor**. To **Exit** out of the **Story Editor**: *File Menu →Close.*

Chapter 4 - Text Threading And Graphics Placement

4.7 Dynamic Spelling	This shows **Red underlines** for **misspelled words** and **Green underlines** for **grammar**. *Edit Menu→Spelling→☑ Enable Dynamic Spelling*.	
4.8 Text Wrap	This will wrap text around a graphic object. Open Panel: *Window Menu→Text Wrap.* Apply Word Wrap: *Select the graphic image→ Apply one of the following:* ▪ - No Text Wrap. ▪ - Wrap around bounding box. *Used Most* ▪ - Wrap around object shape. If you save the object as a transparent object (.gif or .png), the text will wrap around the object. See the **Text Wrap** parameter to the right. ▪ - Jump object. Space to the left or right. ▪ - Jump to next column.	You apply text wrap to the object, not the text.
Practice Exercise 21	Continue from previous exercise. *File Menu→Place→House2 Transparent.png→Open→Place on text.* *Select Image→Text Wrap Panel→* ▪ *Wrap around object shape→ Wrap to: Right Side→Type: Detect Edges.*	
4.9 Alignment Panel	This will align multiple selected objects. *Window Menu→ Object&Layout→Align.*	
4.10 Corner Options	This defines the corner style of the frames. *Select Object→Object Menu→Corner Options→Choose the rounded style.* Rounded Corner Option.	
4.11 Live Corners CS5+	This is an automatic way to round the corners of the frame. Click on the yellow box once, then adjust the corner	
4.12 Text Overset	You will see a **red plus sign** in the lower left corner of the text frame similar to the following: This indicates that the text does not fit in the text frame. Note: To see the hidden text, open the **Story Editor** and page down to the bottom of the text. The hidden text is indicated by a red line located on the left side of the **Story Editor** screen.	
Practice Exercise 22	*Select the text frame→Objects Menu→Text Frame Options→Inset Spacing: 1p0*	

Chapter 4 - Text Threading And Graphics Placement

4.13 Bullets and Number	Paragraph Options: Bulleted List , Numbered List .	• Ruby Tuesday • Olive Garden • Applebee's
4.14 Add a Custom Bullet	Choose the dropdown on the far-right side of the Text options. ***Type Tool→More Options →Numbers and Bullets→Choose new bullet***. *Note:* More options are located on the far-right side of the screen.	
4.15 Indent Bullet	This can be used to indent text or list bullets. Select the bullets→ Left Indent 0p4	
4.16 Drop Cap	Paragraph Option: **Drop Cap** number of lines 0 **Drop Cap** one or more characters. 0	
4.17 Rotate / Transform	*Select Object →Object Menu→Transform→Rotate.*	
4.18 Column Break	This will break and display the information on the top of the next column. ***Type Menu→Insert Break Character→Column Break.***	

Section 2: Optional Concepts

4.19 Table	Insert table, Convert, Options, Insert, Delete, Select, Merge, Split, Convert to, and Distribute. ***Text Tool→Draw Box→Table Menu→Insert Table.***	
4.20 Inset Spacing	This adjusts the text inside the frame: *Select text frame→Object Menu→Text Frame Options→See the Inset Spacing.*	

Student Project B - Healthy Dining Selections

1. **Open InDesign.**
2. **Create a new document and choose the following options:**

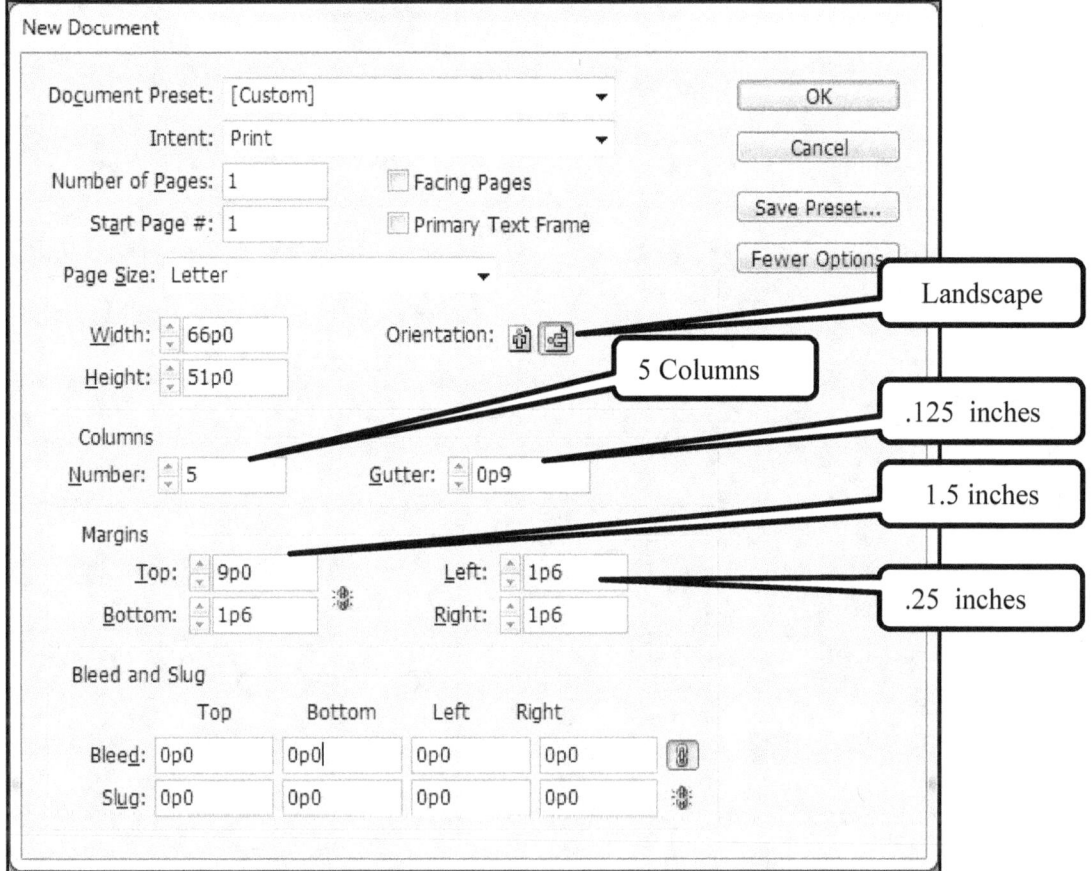

3. The graphic files are located in the InDesignCC-All folder and they start with the letter "B."
   Use the *File Menu→Place* command to place graphic images.

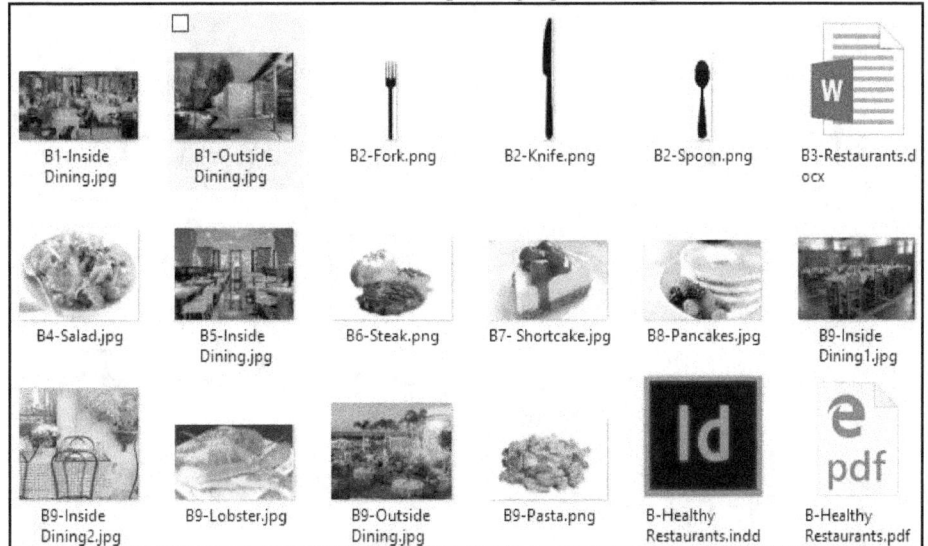

4. Use the *File Menu→Place* command to place text using the file: **B4-Restaurants.docx**

Chapter 4 - Text Threading And Graphics Placement

5. Create the following layout using the text and graphic images.

The completed version is called: **C:\Data\InDesignCC-1\B-Healthy Restaurants.pdf**
Note: This project should take about 30-45 minutes to complete.

Chapter 5 - Master Page

The **Master Page** layout is a commonly misunderstood concept to new InDesign users. It is a fundamental building block and is used to define a background image to be applied to one or all pages. The background information may include a graphic watermark, text labels, page header and footer, page numbers, or anything that you don't want to put on the main pages.

Chapter Contents:
        Section 1: Core Concepts
        Section 2: Optional Concepts

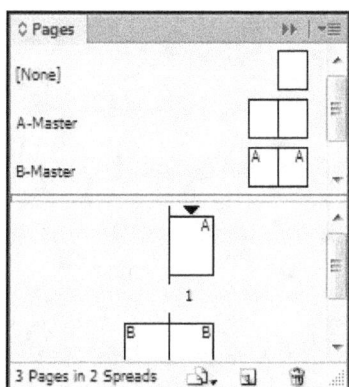

Section 1: Core Concepts

Concept	Explanation / *Command String in italic.*
Practice Exercise 23 Open New Document	Open Blank Document: *File Menu→New→Document→ Document Preset: Default.*
5.1 Page Panel	The **Page Panel** is used to see all pages in a single interface. Also, you can create **Master Pages** that appear as different layers underneath the page. *Window Menu→Page Panel.* Mac CS6: *called the* **Pages Panel**.
5.2 Create Master Page	**Master Pages** appear under the page but not editable on the page. *R-Click in Master page area→New Master.* *Or Select the A-Master →Click the New Page Icon.*
5.3 Delete One Of The Facing Pages	If you only need one of two facing pages, this will allow you to delete the one that is not needed. ***R-Click on the left A-Master Page →Delete Master Page or drag to the Trash can.*** Mac: *Click on A-Master page→More Options →Master Options for A-Master.*
5.4 Change a Master Name	To modify the **Master Page** name, right click on it, and choose **Master Options for "A-Master."**

Chapter 5 - Master Page

5.5 Apply Master To Master	The information in the master will be displayed on the **B-Master**. Drag the **A-Master** on top of the **B-Master**.	*Drag Here.*
5.6 Apply Master To Page 1	Once you create the **Master Pages,** you can apply them to a single page. Drag **A-Master** on top of Page 1.	*Page 1.*
5.7 Create A "New Page"	This is used to create additional pages. *R-Click in the lower page →Insert Pages* or *Click in the lower area and choose the New Page button* . **Mac:** *Select a page in the lower section →Create New Page Icon* .	*New Page.*
5.8 Place graphic On Master	When you place a graphic image on a Master Page, it will appear behind the page. Click on the master page and *File Menu →Place →Graphic Image.* Verify that the lower left corner page name says "A-Master." To format the object to be more transparent: *Select Object →Object Menu →Effects →Transparency → Set Opacity to 25%.*	*Transparent Image.*
5.9 Add A Text Box To A Master	Text boxes added to the **Master Page** will appear on applied pages. 1. Click on B-Master (Verify the lower left corner page name says B-Master). 2. Add a text box on the bottom edge of the page in the margin area. 3. Type in the following: Designed by: (Your Name). Designed By: Jeff Hutchinson	
5.10 Add Page Numbers	**Page Numbers** can be added to the **Master Page** and applied to the desired pages. To add **Page Numbers**, you must first add a text box. Once the **Page Number** is created, you can use the standard formatting features to produce the desired results. 1. Place a text box on the lower outer edge of the margin. 2. Type the word: "**Page**" in both boxes. 3. *Type Menu →Insert Special Character → Markers →Current Page Number* 4. Format the text on the Right side to be **Right Justified**. 5. Format the text on the Left side to be **Left Justified**.	Page A

Chapter 5 - Master Page

Section 2: Optional Concepts

Practice Exercise 24 *Greeting Card*	Create a greeting card: 1. *File Menu→New→Document→Number of Page: 3 →* ☑ *Facing Pages→Width: 5.5in→Height: 4.25in→* *Columns: 1→Margin all: .125 in.* 2. To create a 4 page spread only: *R-Click on page 1 in the Pages Panel→* Allow Document Pages to Shuffle *→ R-Click on page 1 →* *Insert Pages→Insert: Page before.* *Mac CS6: Click on Page 1→More Options →* Allow Document Pages to Shuffle
5.11 Export	*File Menu→Export→Save as Type: Adobe PDF (Print)→Ok.*
5.12 Preflight	This is used to review font and image problems. Errors will be displayed in the status bar.

Practice Exercise 25 - Master Pages (Single Page)
1. Create a new portrait, letter size document and turn off "☐ Facing Pages."
2. Create the following master pages and Link B-Master to A-Master:

3. Do the following to the A-Master:
Place a text box in the center under the lower margin→Type the word: "**Page**." Then use the menu: *Type Menu→Insert Special Character→ Markers→ Current Page Number.*
4. Do the following to the B-Master:
Place a Graphic Image on a B-Master Page and make it transparent.
5. Add pages and apply masters to pages:
Add Pages 1, 2, 3, and 4 in the lower portion of the Page Panel.
Apply A-Master to Page 1 and B-Master to page 2, 3, and 4.

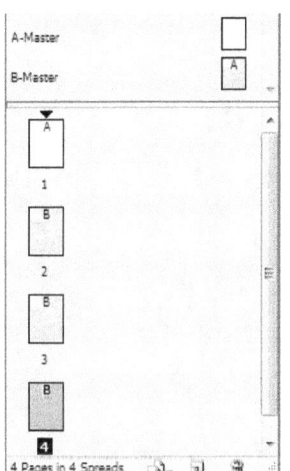

Practice Exercise 26 - Master Pages (Facing Pages)
1. **Create the following new document with facing pages:** *File Menu→New→Document*
Number of Pages: 1
☑ Facing Pages
Page Size: Letter
Width: 51p0
Height: 66p0
Orientation: Portrait
Columns: 2

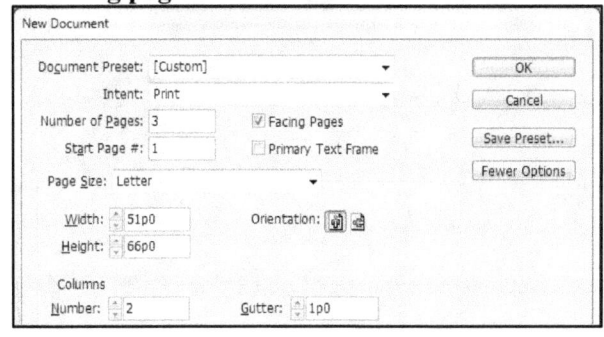

Chapter 5 - Master Page

2. Create the following Master pages:

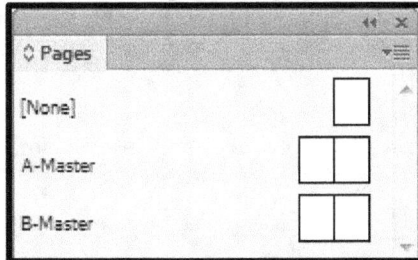

3. Place an image across the facing pages of A-Master and format it to be Transparent.
File Menu→Place→ B-House1.jpg →Place on A Master →Select image →
Object Menu →Effects →Transparency →Opacity: 22%.

4. Place a text box on the lower outer edge of the B-Master.
5. Type the word: Page.
6. *Type Menu →Insert Special Character →Markers →Current Page Number.*

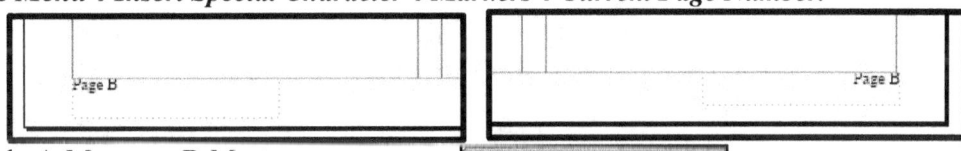

7. Apply A-Master to B-Master.

8. Apply A-Master to page 1.

9. Apply B-Master to pages 2 and 3.

10. View the document to see the results.

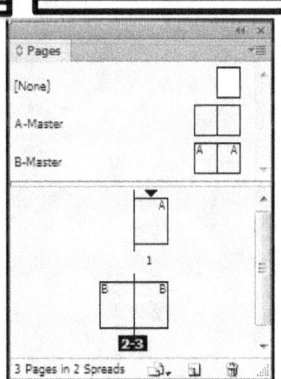

Student Project C - Four Page Newsletter

Note: The final project file name is "C5-Healthy Lifestyles.pdf."

1. ***Open InDesign and start a new blank document with the following parameters:***
   File Menu→New→Document.

   Number of Pages: 4
   ☑ Facing Pages
   Page Size: Letter
   Width: 51p0
   Height: 66p0
   Orientation: Portrait
   Columns: 1

   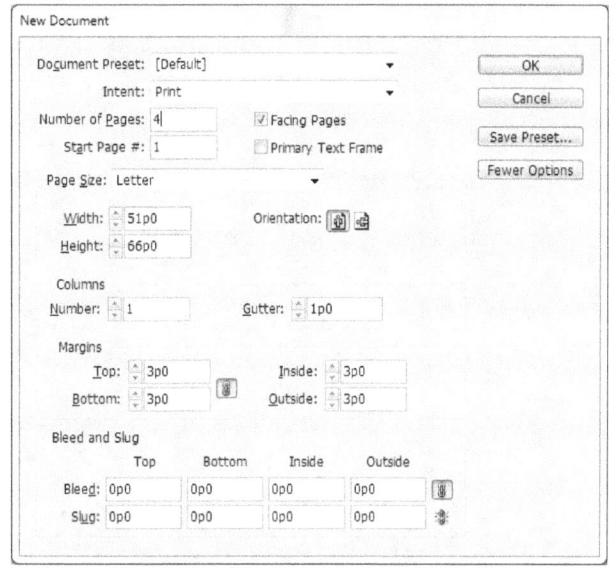

2. **A-Header/Footer Master**
   Create the following text box on the **A-Header/Footer Master** and place the current page marker.

   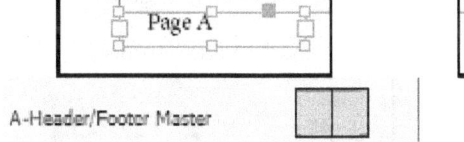

   Place the Left and Right banner on the top of the page.
   File Menu→Place→G0-Left Banner.jpg   *File Menu→Place→G0-Right Banner.jpg.*

3. **B-Title Page Master**
   Create the B-Title Page Master.
   Delete page one of the B-Title Page Master.

   Change the Margins: ***Layout Menu→Margin and Columns*** Note:
   Break the link for the top margin. Top: 2 in, Bottom: .5 in.

   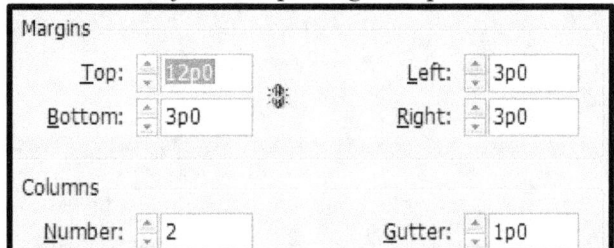

4. **C-2 Column Master**
   Create C-2 Column Master.
   Apply A-Header/Footer to C-2 Column Master.

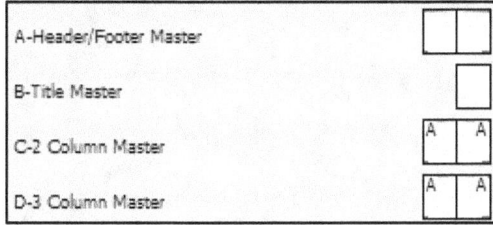

Format the columns to 2: *Layout Menu→Margin and columns→Column=2*.

5. **D-3 Column Master**

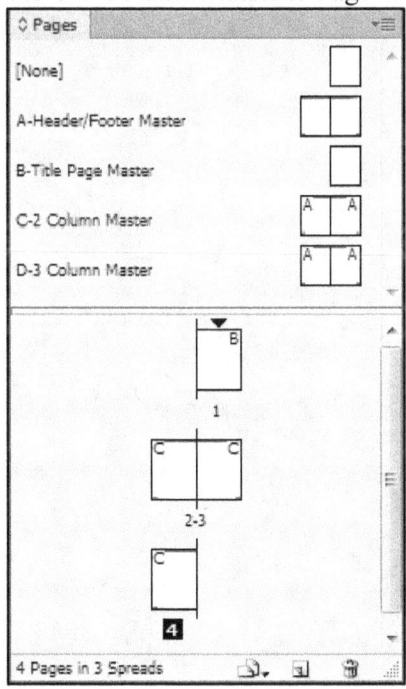

Apply A-Header/Footer Master to D-3 Column Master.

Format the columns to 3: *Layout Menu→Margin and columns→Column=3*.

6. **Apply Masters to Each Page**

Apply the B-Title Page Master to Page 1.
Apply the C-2 Column Master to Page 2.
Apply the C-2 Column Master to Page 3.
Apply the C-2 Column Master to Page 4.

7. **Design Page 1 using the following graphic files:**

C1-Balanced Diet.docx

C1-Healthy Life Exit.png

C1-Scale.png

C1-What is a Healthy Lifestyle.docx

8. **Design Page 2 using the following graphic files:**

C2-Good Vs.docx

C2-The Truth about Calories.docx

C2-Fish.png

C2-Fruits.png

C2-Grains.png

C2-Meat.png

C2-Pasta.png

C2-Salad.png

C2-Steak.png

C2-Vegetables.png

Guide to a Healthy Lifestyle

What is a Healthy Lifestyle?

We all want to live a long, happy, healthy life with an abundance of energy and vitality. We want to have the ability to perform well both mentally and physically with emotional balance and be free from disease and disorders. One may ask, why is a healthy lifestyle important and how can we accomplish a healthy lifestyle with all of today's temptations? To achieve this we need to strive for peak health through a Healthy Lifestyle.

Leading a healthy lifestyle is one of the best decisions you will ever make, one which will impact on all aspects of your life – physical, mental, and emotional. A healthy lifestyle is a valuable resource for reducing the incidence and impact of health problems, enabling you better to cope with life stressors, as well as improving your quality of life.

Many health problems can be prevented or at least their occurrence postponed by having a healthy lifestyle. Many health issues are addressed with exercise, nutrition, stress management and other healthy lifestyle practices.

No matter what your age or where you are in your life today, it is never too late to improve your lifestyle to make the most of your health and well-being. Developing and maintaining a healthy lifestyle will change your life for the better.

Balanced Diet

Everyone knows that eating a healthy balanced diet, exercising regularly and coping with stress can be beneficial to the body and mind, and are habits necessary for a healthy lifestyle. But, how do you balance work and family, and all the other areas of your life without spreading yourself too thin, then developing a guilt trip when you do one thing, but think you should be doing another? The solution is to incorporate a healthy lifestyle plan that is designed to ensure you have your life in balance.

A healthy lifestyle must create personal well-being – or to put it another way, enable you to balance things in your daily life. All of the key areas of our lives overlap and interlink, affecting each other. Unless we create for ourselves satisfaction in each and every part of our life, we can never truly be fulfilled, or live a contented, happy and healthy life.

The key is to make these healthy lifestyle habits part of your everyday life. You will need to change your existing everyday habits in order to adopt and maintain your new healthy lifestyle. This new lifestyle will allow you to obtain the healthy lifestyle goals you want. You will experience a major change in your life; you will become stronger, sexier, and feel great. Good healthy lifestyle habits will include the following:

- Eating correctly.
- Exercising sufficiently.
- Using your mind effectively.
- Limiting unnecessary stress.

Good Vs. Bad Cholesterol

It may surprise you to know that not all cholesterol is bad for you. In fact, cholesterol is just one of the many substances created and used by our bodies to keep us healthy. Some of the cholesterol we need is produced naturally, while some of it comes from the food we eat.

There are two types of cholesterol, the "good" and the "bad". It is important to understand the difference and know the levels of each in your blood. Too much of one, or not enough of another, can put you at risk for coronary heart disease, heart attack or stroke.

LDL (Bad) Cholesterol

If you have too much of this cholesterol in the blood, it will build up in the inner walls of the arteries that feed the heart and brain. When the arteries begin to narrow, heart attack or stroke can result. Avoid saturated and trans fats, as they are believed to increase LDL levels.

HDL (Good) Cholesterol

High levels of HDL in the blood protect against heart attack. HDL carries cholesterol away from the arteries and back to the liver, where it is passed from the body. Regular physical activity has been known to increase HDL levels.

Page 2

The Truth about Calories

For years now, calories have been all the rage. People are counting them and cutting them, and you'd be hard-pressed to find something at the supermarket that does not list its calories per serving somewhere on the package. Calories, or food energy, refer to the amount of energy obtained from food. There are many variables that determine how many calories men and women should consume each day.

In recent years, the tides have turned away from the simplistic "calories in versus calories out" approach to weight loss. In 2011, a long-term follow-up study involving more than 120,000 non-obese individuals was released; it was by far the most exhaustive study of its kind, following these men and women for up to 20 years and meticulously recording their weights And, to popular contrary the study opinion, that the showed food you eat matter quite a bit — so yes, it matters types of where your calories come from. Dr. Dariush Mozaf-

farian of the Harvard School of Public Health and lead author of the study says, "What you eat makes quite a difference. Just counting calories won't matter much unless you look at the kinds of calories you're eating."

9. **Design Page 3 using the following graphic files:**

C3-Benefits of Regular Exercise.docx

C3-Biking.png

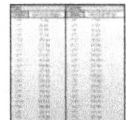
C3-BMI Chart.png

C3-Exercise.png

C3-Runner.png

C3-What is BMI.docx

10. **Design Page 4 using the following Graphic files:**

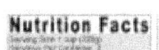

C4-1Nutrition Facts.png C4-2Per Serving.png C4-3Total Fat.png

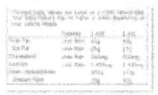

C4-4Fiber.png C4-5Footnote.png C4-Understanding Food Labels.docx

What is BMI?

BMI (Body Mass Index) is a tool used to measure weight relative to height. This tool is used as an accurate alternative to body fat measurement, and can provide insight to your overall health.

Use the chart to determine ideal weight.

Benefits of Regular Exercise

We all know that exercise on a regular basis is good for us; but, what are the specific benefits we can expect to gain from it? Listed below are six specific ways exercise can improve your life.

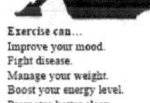

Exercise can...
Improve your mood.
Fight disease.
Manage your weight.
Boost your energy level.
Promotes better sleep.
Add fun to your daily routine.

Convinced yet? Remember, exercise is all about moving. You don't have to go for a 10 mile run to exercise. Start small, and incorporate things you enjoy into your routine. Take your dog for a walk, go for a swim, take dancing lessons, play tennis, etc. Now get moving!

Page 3

The Nutrition Facts Label

People look at food labels for different reasons. But whatever the reason, many consumers would like to know how to use this information more effectively and easily. The following is intended to make it easier for you to use nutrition labels for quick, informed food choices that contribute to a healthy diet.

The five main components in a nutrition label are: serving size, calories, total fat, Vitamins, and Daily Values.

The Serving Size

The first place to start when looking at the Nutrition Facts label is the serving size and the number of servings in the package. The size of the serving on the food package influences the number of calories and all the nutrient amounts listed on the top part of the label. In the sample label, one serving of macaroni and cheese equals one cup. If you ate the whole package, you would eat two cups. That doubles the calories and other nutrient numbers, including the %Daily Values as shown in the sample label.

Calories (and Calories from Fat)

Calories provide a measure of how much energy you get from a serving of this food. Many Americans consume more calories than they need without meeting recommended intakes for a number of nutrients. The calorie section of the label can help you manage your weight (i.e., gain, lose, or maintain.) Remember: the number of servings you consume determines the number of calories you actually eat (your portion amount).
In the sample label, there are 250 calories in one serving of this macaroni and cheese. How many calories from fat are there in ONE serving? Answer: 110 calories, which means almost half the calories in a single serving come from fat. What if you ate the whole package content? Then, you would consume two servings, or 500 calories, and 220 would come from fat.

Total Fat (Limit these Nutrients)

Look at the top of the nutrient section in the sample label. It shows some key nutrients that impact your health and separates them into two main groups.

The nutrients listed first are the ones Americans generally eat in adequate amounts, or even too much. Eating too much fat, saturated fat, trans fat, cholesterol, or sodium may increase your risk of certain chronic diseases, like heart disease, some cancers, or high blood pressure.

Vitamins

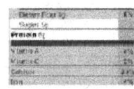

Most Americans don't get enough dietary fiber, vitamin A, vitamin C, calcium, and iron in their diets. Eating enough of these nutrients can improve health and help reduce the risk of some diseases and conditions. For example, getting enough calcium may reduce the risk of osteoporosis, a condition that results in brittle bones as one ages (see calcium section). Eating a diet high in dietary fiber promotes healthy bowel function. Additionally, a diet rich in fruits, vegetables, and grain products that contain dietary fiber, particularly soluble fiber, and low in saturated fat and cholesterol may reduce the risk of heart disease.

Daily Values

The footnote on the bottom part of the label contains a footnote with Daily Values (DV's) for 2,000 and 2,500 calorie diets. This footnote provides recommended dietary information for important nutrients including fats, sodium and fiber. This statement must be on all food labels except if the package size is too small.

Page 4

Student Project C - Four Page Newsletter

11. Export to PDF: *File Menu→Export→Save as Type: Adobe PDF (Print)→Ok.*

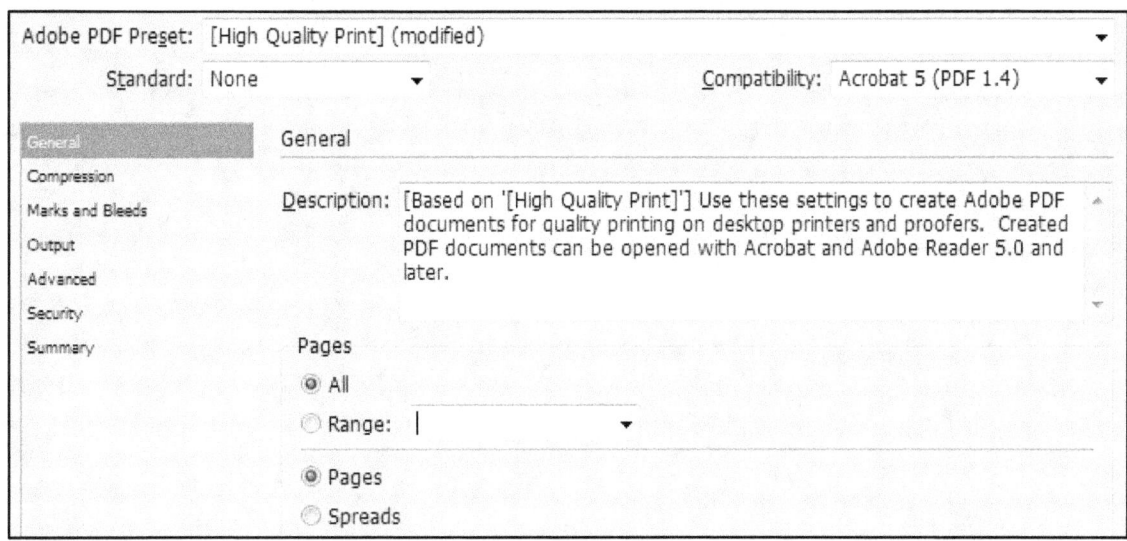

Index - InDesign CC Creating Brochures

Accelerate..................... 10
Accelerate Movement..... 10
Add a Custom Bullet....... 18
Add a text box to a Master 22
Add Page Numbers......... 22
Alignment Panel.............. 17
Application Bar................ 7
Automatic Text Threading 16
Bleed................... 13
Bullets and Number........ 18
Change a master name... 21
Color Panel...................... 9
Color Picker..................... 9
Column Break................. 18
Column Master.......... 25, 26
Columns.......................... 13
Control Panel................... 5
Converting Shapes.......... 10
Copy Frame..................... 9
Corner Options................ 17
Create a new page........... 22
Create Master page......... 21
Current Page Number.... 22
Delete one of the facing Pages............................ 21
Dictionary.................... 7, 10
Direct Selection tool......... 6
DisplayPerformance... 7, 10
Document Presets............ 12
Document Window............ 5
Drop Cap......................... 18
Dynamic Spelling............. 17
Ellipse Tool....................... 8
Export............................... 23
Export to PDF.................. 29

Eye Dropper..................... 10
Facing Pages................... 12
Fewer/More Options....... 13
Fit a Frame...................... 10
Frame Handles................. 9
Frames.............................. 8
Graphics Placement........ 16
Grouping Objects............ 10
Guides.............................. 6
Hand Tool......................... 8
Inches Vs Pica................. 14
Indent Bullet.................... 18
Inset Spacing................... 18
Intent............................... 12
Keyboard........................... 5
Line Tool........................... 8
Link Master to Master.... 22
Link Page 1 to Master..... 22
Live Corners.................... 17
Mac vs Windows............... 4
Manual Text Threading.. 16
Margins........................... 13
Master Page..................... 21
Masters............................ 23
Menu................................. 5
Menu Bar.......................... 5
New Document................ 12
Number of pages............. 12
Page Panel....................... 21
Page Size......................... 13
Panels............................... 5
Perspective....................... 9
Pica.................................. 13
Place graphic on Master. 22
Placing Text/Graphics...... 8
Polygon Tool..................... 8
Preferences....................... 6

Preflight........................... 23
Rectangle Tool.................. 8
Redo.................................. 6
Rotate.......................... 9, 18
Rulers............................... 6
Save Preset..................... 12
Screen Mode................... 10
Selection......................... 16
Selection Tool................... 6
Simi-Automatic Text Threading.................... 16
Slug................................. 14
Smart Guides.................... 7
Special Characters............ 9
Stacking Order................ 10
Start Page....................... 12
Story Editor.................... 16
Strokes Panel.................... 9
Swatches Panel................. 9
Table................................ 18
Terminology...................... 4
Text Frame Options......... 9
Text Overset.................... 17
Text Threading................ 16
Text Wrap........................ 17
Thread between Text Boxes 16
Title Page Master............ 25
Tools Panel........................ 5
Type on a Path.................. 8
Type Tool.......................... 8
Undo.................................. 6
Vertical Justification......... 9
View Commands............... 6
Workspace........................ 5
Zoom Tool......................... 8
Zooming............................ 6